2020 RESELLER ACCOUNTING LEDGER

By Ann Eckhart

2020 RESELLER ACCOUNTING LEDGER

Copyright © 2019 by Ann Eckhart

Cover Design by Ann Eckhart

This book is not intended as a
substitute for the professional
accounting and tax advice of a CPA.

I have been selling online – specifically on Ebay, but also on Amazon, Etsy, and Poshmark - since 2005; and in this book, you'll find the same bookkeeping record style that I've used from the beginning! Detailing your business expenses is essential come tax time; and this workbook makes keeping track of those costs super easy. Every month features a monthly calendar along with a Bank Account ledger, Mileage ledger, and Cost of Goods ledger. Each month ends with an Income Report sheet for your gross sales and total expenses. Subtract your expenses from your gross sales and you'll have your NET profit for each month.

The last page of this book is your Year-End Income Report. Simply add up your gross sales from every month and then add up each monthly expense category. Subtract your total yearly expenses from your total yearly gross sales to see how much net profit you actually made this year. This year-end sheet is the only one I give to my accountant come tax time (along with any tax forms I've been issued from the sites I sell on).

Note that whether or not you receive a tax form from the sites you sell on varies by platform. However, even if you aren't issued a tax form, you STILL need to file taxes on your earnings. Please remember that this book is a tool to help you in your business; it does not replace the professional advice of a CPA.

I hope this book helps you with your reselling accounting! Here's to a successful and profitable year on whichever platforms you sell!

Happy Selling!
Ann Eckhart

HOW TO USE THE LEDGERS IN THIS BOOK

The ledgers in this book work just like the checkbook ledgers you likely already use in your personal life. Keeping up with these entries means you'll be able to easily calculate your monthly and year-end Income Report totals.

BANK ACCOUNT LEDGER:
- Check # (number on the check, if one was written)
- Date (date of the transaction)
- Transaction (nature or location, i.e. "Goodwill", "PayPal", or "Postage")
- Debit (amount of money spent/withdrawn; you'll be referencing your debits at the end of every month when you categorize your expenses)
OR
- Credit (amount of money deposited)
- Balance (running bank account balance)

MILEAGE LEDGER:
- Date (date of car trip)
- Destination (where you drove to)
- Task (nature of the trip, i.e. "sourcing" or "Post Office")
- Miles (total round-trip miles for specific trip)
- Total (running balance of all miles for the month)

COST OF GOODS:
- Date (date when goods to resell were purchased)
- Location (where goods were purchased)
- Cash/Check/Card (your method of payment)
- Cost (amount spent at specific location)
- Total (running balance of your COG's for the month)

2020 FEDERAL HOLIDAYS
NO MAIL & POST OFFICES CLOSED

Wednesay, January 1 - New Year's Day

Monday, January 20 - Martin Luther King Jr. Birthday

Monday, February 17 - Washington's Birthday (President's Day)

Monday, May 25 - Memorial Day

Friday, July 3 & Saturday, July 4 - Independence Day (no mail Saturday and some post office locations may also be closed Friday)

Monday, September 7 - Labor Day

Monday, Octobevr 12 - Columbus Day

Wednesday, November 11 - Veteran's Day

Thursday, November 26 - Thanksgiving Day

Friday, December 25 - Christmas Day

2020

January

S	M	T	W	T	F	S
			1	2	3	4
5	6	7	8	9	10	11
12	13	14	15	16	17	18
19	20	21	22	23	24	25
26	27	28	29	30	31	

February

S	M	T	W	T	F	S
						1
2	3	4	5	6	7	8
9	10	11	12	13	14	15
16	17	18	19	20	21	22
23	24	25	26	27	28	29

March

S	M	T	W	T	F	S
1	2	3	4	5	6	7
8	9	10	11	12	13	14
15	16	17	18	19	20	21
22	23	24	25	26	27	28
29	30	31				

April

S	M	T	W	T	F	S
			1	2	3	4
5	6	7	8	9	10	11
12	13	14	15	16	17	18
19	20	21	22	23	24	25
26	27	28	29	30		

May

S	M	T	W	T	F	S
					1	2
3	4	5	6	7	8	9
10	11	12	13	14	15	16
17	18	19	20	21	22	23
24	25	26	27	28	29	30
31						

June

S	M	T	W	T	F	S
	1	2	3	4	5	6
7	8	9	10	11	12	13
14	15	16	17	18	19	20
21	22	23	24	25	26	27
28	29	30				

July

S	M	T	W	T	F	S
			1	2	3	4
5	6	7	8	9	10	11
12	13	14	15	16	17	18
19	20	21	22	23	24	25
26	27	28	29	30	31	

August

S	M	T	W	T	F	S
						1
2	3	4	5	6	7	8
9	10	11	12	13	14	15
16	17	18	19	20	21	22
23	24	25	26	27	28	29
30	31					

September

S	M	T	W	T	F	S
		1	2	3	4	5
6	7	8	9	10	11	12
13	14	15	16	17	18	19
20	21	22	23	24	25	26
27	28	29	30			

October

S	M	T	W	T	F	S
			1	2	3	
4	5	6	7	8	9	10
11	12	13	14	15	16	17
18	19	20	21	22	23	24
25	26	27	28	29	30	31

November

S	M	T	W	T	F	S
1	2	3	4	5	6	7
8	9	10	11	12	13	14
15	16	17	18	19	20	21
22	23	24	25	26	27	28
29	30					

December

S	M	T	W	T	F	S
		1	2	3	4	5
6	7	8	9	10	11	12
13	14	15	16	17	18	19
20	21	22	23	24	25	26
27	28	29	30	31		

JANUARY 2020

LISTING GOALS

ACTUAL LISTINGS

SALES GOALS

ACTUAL SALES

NOTES:

January 2020

Sunday	Monday	Tuesday	Wednesday	Thursday	Friday	Saturday
29	30	31	1	2	3	4
5	6	7	8	9	10	11
12	13	14	15	16	17	18
19	20	21	22	23	24	25
26	27	28	29	30	31	1

JANUARY BANK ACCOUNT LEDGER

CHECK #	DATE	TRANSACTION	DEBIT	CREDIT	BALANCE

JANUARY BANK ACCOUNT LEDGER

CHECK #	DATE	TRANSACTION	DEBIT	CREDIT	BALANCE

JANUARY MILEAGE

DATE	DESTINATION	TASK	MILES	TOTAL

JANUARY MILEAGE

DATE	DESTINATION	TASK	MILES	TOTAL

JANUARY COST OF GOODS (COGS)

DATE	LOCATION	CASH/CHECK/CARD	COST	TOTAL

JANUARY COST OF GOODS (COGS)

DATE	LOCATION	CASH/CHECK/CARD	COST	TOTAL

JANUARY INCOME REPORT
GROSS SALES

Amazon Sales:

Ebay Sales:

Etsy Sales:

Poshmark Sales:

Mercari Sales:

Facebook Sales:

Instagram Sales:

YouTube Sales:

Local Sales:

Other Sales:

TOTAL JANUARY GROSS SALES:

JANUARY INCOME REPORT - EXPENSES

Amazon Fees:
Ebay Fees:
Etsy Fees:
Poshmark Fees:
Mercari Fees:
PayPal Fees:
Additional Fees:

Cost of Goods:
Postage:
Advertising:
Office/Shipping Supplies:
Equipment:
Phone/Internet:

Sales Tax:
Business Insurance:
Health Insurance Premiums:
Prescription Drugs:
CoPays/Deductibles:

Travel:
Meals:
Additional Expenses:

TOTAL JANUARY EXPENSES:

JANUARY NET PROFIT:
(Gross Sales Minus Expenses)

JANUARY MILEAGE:

FEBRUARY 2020

LISTING GOALS

ACTUAL LISTINGS

SALES GOALS

ACTUAL SALES

NOTES:

February 2020

Sunday	Monday	Tuesday	Wednesday	Thursday	Friday	Saturday
26	27	28	29	30	31	1
2	3	4	5	6	7	8
9	10	11	12	13	14	15
16	17	18	19	20	21	22
23	24	25	26	27	28	29

_____

_____

_____

_____

FEBRUARY BANK ACCOUNT LEDGER

CHECK #	DATE	TRANSACTION	DEBIT	CREDIT	BALANCE

FEBRUARY BANK ACCOUNT LEDGER

CHECK #	DATE	TRANSACTION	DEBIT	CREDIT	BALANCE

FEBRUARY MILEAGE

DATE	DESTINATION	TASK	MILES	TOTAL

FEBRUARY MILEAGE

DATE	DESTINATION	TASK	MILES	TOTAL

FEBRUARY COST OF GOODS (COGS)

DATE	LOCATION	CASH/CHECK/CARD	COST	TOTAL

FEBRUARY COST OF GOODS (COGS)

DATE	LOCATION	CASH/CHECK/CARD	COST	TOTAL

FEBRUARY INCOME REPORT
GROSS SALES

Amazon Sales:

Ebay Sales:

Etsy Sales:

Poshmark Sales:

Mercari Sales:

Facebook Sales:

Instagram Sales:

YouTube Sales:

Local Sales:

Other Sales:

TOTAL FEBRUARY GROSS SALES:

FEBRUARY INCOME REPORT - EXPENSES

Amazon Fees:
Ebay Fees:
Etsy Fees:
Poshmark Fees:
Mercari Fees:
PayPal Fees:
Additional Fees:

Cost of Goods:
Postage:
Advertising:
Office/Shipping Supplies:
Equipment:
Phone/Internet:

Sales Tax:
Business Insurance:
Health Insurance Premiums:
Prescription Drugs:
CoPays/Deductibles:

Travel:
Meals:
Additional Expenses:

TOTAL FEBRUARY EXPENSES:

FEBRUARY NET PROFIT:
(Gross Sales Minus Expenses)

FEBRUARY MILEAGE:

MARCH 2020

LISTING GOALS

ACTUAL LISTINGS

SALES GOALS

ACTUAL SALES

NOTES:

March 2020

Sunday	Monday	Tuesday	Wednesday	Thursday	Friday	Saturday
1	2	3	4	5	6	7
8	9	10	11	12	13	14
15	16	17	18	19	20	21
22	23	24	25	26	27	28
29	30	31	1	2	3	4

MARCH BANK ACCOUNT LEDGER

CHECK #	DATE	TRANSACTION	DEBIT	CREDIT	BALANCE

MARCH BANK ACCOUNT LEDGER

CHECK #	DATE	TRANSACTION	DEBIT	CREDIT	BALANCE

MARCH MILEAGE

DATE	DESTINATION	TASK	MILES	TOTAL

MARCH MILEAGE

DATE	DESTINATION	TASK	MILES	TOTAL

MARCH COST OF GOODS (COGS)

DATE	LOCATION	CASH/CHECK/CARD	COST	TOTAL

MARCH COST OF GOODS (COGS)

DATE	LOCATION	CASH/CHECK/CARD	COST	TOTAL

MARCH INCOME REPORT
GROSS SALES

Amazon Sales:

Ebay Sales:

Etsy Sales:

Poshmark Sales:

Mercari Sales:

Facebook Sales:

Instagram Sales:

YouTube Sales:

Local Sales:

Other Sales:

TOTAL MARCH GROSS SALES:

MARCH INCOME REPORT - EXPENSES

Amazon Fees:
Ebay Fees:
Etsy Fees:
Poshmark Fees:
Mercari Fees:
PayPal Fees:
Additional Fees:

Cost of Goods:
Postage:
Advertising:
Office/Shipping Supplies:
Equipment:
Phone/Internet:

Sales Tax:
Business Insurance:
Health Insurance Premiums:
Prescription Drugs:
CoPays/Deductibles:

Travel:
Meals:
Additional Expenses:

TOTAL MARCH EXPENSES:

MARCH NET PROFIT:
(Gross Sales Minus Expenses)

MARCH MILEAGE:

APRIL 2020

LISTING GOALS

ACTUAL LISTINGS

SALES GOALS

ACTUAL SALES

NOTES:

April 2020

Sunday	Monday	Tuesday	Wednesday	Thursday	Friday	Saturday
29	30	31	1	2	3	4
5	6	7	8	9	10	11
12	13	14	15	16	17	18
19	20	21	22	23	24	25
26	27	28	29	30	1	2

APRIL BANK ACCOUNT LEDGER

CHECK #	DATE	TRANSACTION	DEBIT	CREDIT	BALANCE

APRIL BANK ACCOUNT LEDGER

CHECK #	DATE	TRANSACTION	DEBIT	CREDIT	BALANCE

APRIL MILEAGE

DATE	DESTINATION	TASK	MILES	TOTAL

APRIL MILEAGE

DATE	DESTINATION	TASK	MILES	TOTAL

APRIL COST OF GOODS (COGS)

DATE	LOCATION	CASH/CHECK/CARD	COST	TOTAL

APRIL COST OF GOODS (COGS)

DATE	LOCATION	CASH/CHECK/CARD	COST	TOTAL

APRIL INCOME REPORT
GROSS SALES

Amazon Sales:

Ebay Sales:

Etsy Sales:

Poshmark Sales:

Mercari Sales:

Facebook Sales:

Instagram Sales:

YouTube Sales:

Local Sales:

Other Sales:

TOTAL APRIL GROSS SALES:

APRIL INCOME REPORT - EXPENSES

Amazon Fees:
Ebay Fees:
Etsy Fees:
Poshmark Fees:
Mercari Fees:
PayPal Fees:
Additional Fees:

Cost of Goods:
Postage:
Advertising:
Office/Shipping Supplies:
Equipment:
Phone/Internet:

Sales Tax:
Business Insurance:
Health Insurance Premiums:
Prescription Drugs:
CoPays/Deductibles:

Travel:
Meals:
Additional Expenses:

TOTAL APRIL EXPENSES:

APRIL NET PROFIT:
(Gross Sales Minus Expenses)

APRIL MILEAGE:

MAY 2020

LISTING GOALS

ACTUAL LISTINGS

SALES GOALS

ACTUAL SALES

NOTES:

May 2020

Sunday	Monday	Tuesday	Wednesday	Thursday	Friday	Saturday
26	27	28	29	30	1	2
3	4	5	6	7	8	9
10	11	12	13	14	15	16
17	18	19	20	21	22	23
24	25	26	27	28	29	30
31	1	2	3	4	5	6

MAY BANK ACCOUNT LEDGER

CHECK #	DATE	TRANSACTION	DEBIT	CREDIT	BALANCE

MAY BANK ACCOUNT LEDGER

CHECK #	DATE	TRANSACTION	DEBIT	CREDIT	BALANCE

MAY MILEAGE

DATE	DESTINATION	TASK	MILES	TOTAL

MAY MILEAGE

DATE	DESTINATION	TASK	MILES	TOTAL

MAY COST OF GOODS (COGS)

DATE	LOCATION	CASH/CHECK/CARD	COST	TOTAL

MAY COST OF GOODS (COGS)

DATE	LOCATION	CASH/CHECK/CARD	COST	TOTAL

MAY INCOME REPORT
GROSS SALES

Amazon Sales:

Ebay Sales:

Etsy Sales:

Poshmark Sales:

Mercari Sales:

Facebook Sales:

Instagram Sales:

YouTube Sales:

Local Sales:

Other Sales:

TOTAL MAY GROSS SALES:

MAY INCOME REPORT - EXPENSES

Amazon Fees:
Ebay Fees:
Etsy Fees:
Poshmark Fees:
Mercari Fees:
PayPal Fees:
Additional Fees:

Cost of Goods:
Postage:
Advertising:
Office/Shipping Supplies:
Equipment:
Phone/Internet:

Sales Tax:
Business Insurance:
Health Insurance Premiums:
Prescription Drugs:
CoPays/Deductibles:

Travel:
Meals:
Additional Expenses:

TOTAL MAY EXPENSES:

MAY NET PROFIT:
(Gross Sales Minus Expenses)

MAY MILEAGE:

JUNE 2020

LISTING GOALS

ACTUAL LISTINGS

SALES GOALS

ACTUAL SALES

NOTES:

June 2020

Sunday	Monday	Tuesday	Wednesday	Thursday	Friday	Saturday
31	1	2	3	4	5	6
7	8	9	10	11	12	13
14	15	16	17	18	19	20
21	22	23	24	25	26	27
28	29	30	1	2	3	4

_____
_____
_____
_____

JUNE BANK ACCOUNT LEDGER

CHECK #	DATE	TRANSACTION	DEBIT	CREDIT	BALANCE

JUNE BANK ACCOUNT LEDGER

CHECK #	DATE	TRANSACTION	DEBIT	CREDIT	BALANCE

JUNE MILEAGE

DATE	DESTINATION	TASK	MILES	TOTAL

JUNE MILEAGE

DATE	DESTINATION	TASK	MILES	TOTAL

JUNE COST OF GOODS (COGS)

DATE	LOCATION	CASH/CHECK/CARD	COST	TOTAL

JUNE COST OF GOODS (COGS)

DATE	LOCATION	CASH/CHECK/CARD	COST	TOTAL

JUNE INCOME REPORT
GROSS SALES

Amazon Sales:

Ebay Sales:

Etsy Sales:

Poshmark Sales:

Mercari Sales:

Facebook Sales:

Instagram Sales:

YouTube Sales:

Local Sales:

Other Sales:

TOTAL JUNE GROSS SALES:

JUNE INCOME REPORT - EXPENSES

Amazon Fees:
Ebay Fees:
Etsy Fees:
Poshmark Fees:
Mercari Fees:
PayPal Fees:
Additional Fees:

Cost of Goods:
Postage:
Advertising:
Office/Shipping Supplies:
Equipment:
Phone/Internet:

Sales Tax:
Business Insurance:
Health Insurance Premiums:
Prescription Drugs:
CoPays/Deductibles:

Travel:
Meals:
Additional Expenses:

TOTAL JUNE EXPENSES:

JUNE NET PROFIT:
(Gross Sales Minus Expenses)

JUNE MILEAGE:

JULY 2020

LISTING GOALS

ACTUAL LISTINGS

SALES GOALS

ACTUAL SALES

NOTES:

July 2020

Sunday	Monday	Tuesday	Wednesday	Thursday	Friday	Saturday
28	29	30	1	2	3	4
5	6	7	8	9	10	11
12	13	14	15	16	17	18
19	20	21	22	23	24	25
26	27	28	29	30	31	1

JULY BANK ACCOUNT LEDGER

CHECK #	DATE	TRANSACTION	DEBIT	CREDIT	BALANCE

JULY BANK ACCOUNT LEDGER

CHECK #	DATE	TRANSACTION	DEBIT	CREDIT	BALANCE

JULY MILEAGE

DATE	DESTINATION	TASK	MILES	TOTAL

JULY MILEAGE

DATE	DESTINATION	TASK	MILES	TOTAL

JULY COST OF GOODS (COGS)

DATE	LOCATION	CASH/CHECK/CARD	COST	TOTAL

JULY COST OF GOODS (COGS)

DATE	LOCATION	CASH/CHECK/CARD	COST	TOTAL

JULY INCOME REPORT
GROSS SALES

Amazon Sales:

Ebay Sales:

Etsy Sales:

Poshmark Sales:

Mercari Sales:

Facebook Sales:

Instagram Sales:

YouTube Sales:

Local Sales:

Other Sales:

TOTAL JULY GROSS SALES:

JULY INCOME REPORT - EXPENSES

Amazon Fees:
Ebay Fees:
Etsy Fees:
Poshmark Fees:
Mercari Fees:
PayPal Fees:
Additional Fees:

Cost of Goods:
Postage:
Advertising:
Office/Shipping Supplies:
Equipment:
Phone/Internet:

Sales Tax:
Business Insurance:
Health Insurance Premiums:
Prescription Drugs:
CoPays/Deductibles:

Travel:
Meals:
Additional Expenses:

TOTAL JULY EXPENSES:

JULY NET PROFIT:
(Gross Sales Minus Expenses)

JULY MILEAGE:

AUGUST 2020

LISTING GOALS

ACTUAL LISTINGS

SALES GOALS

ACTUAL SALES

NOTES:

August 2020

Sunday	Monday	Tuesday	Wednesday	Thursday	Friday	Saturday
26	27	28	29	30	31	1
2	3	4	5	6	7	8
9	10	11	12	13	14	15
16	17	18	19	20	21	22
23	24	25	26	27	28	29
30	31	1	2	3	4	5

AUGUST BANK ACCOUNT LEDGER

CHECK #	DATE	TRANSACTION	DEBIT	CREDIT	BALANCE

AUGUST BANK ACCOUNT LEDGER

CHECK #	DATE	TRANSACTION	DEBIT	CREDIT	BALANCE

AUGUST MILEAGE

DATE	DESTINATION	TASK	MILES	TOTAL

AUGUST MILEAGE

DATE	DESTINATION	TASK	MILES	TOTAL

AUGUST COST OF GOODS (COGS)

DATE	LOCATION	CASH/CHECK/CARD	COST	TOTAL

AUGUST COST OF GOODS (COGS)

DATE	LOCATION	CASH/CHECK/CARD	COST	TOTAL

AUGUST INCOME REPORT
GROSS SALES

Amazon Sales:

Ebay Sales:

Etsy Sales:

Poshmark Sales:

Mercari Sales:

Facebook Sales:

Instagram Sales:

YouTube Sales:

Local Sales:

Other Sales:

TOTAL AUGUST GROSS SALES:

AUGUST INCOME REPORT - EXPENSES

Amazon Fees:
Ebay Fees:
Etsy Fees:
Poshmark Fees:
Mercari Fees:
PayPal Fees:
Additional Fees:

Cost of Goods:
Postage:
Advertising:
Office/Shipping Supplies:
Equipment:
Phone/Internet:

Sales Tax:
Business Insurance:
Health Insurance Premiums:
Prescription Drugs:
CoPays/Deductibles:

Travel:
Meals:
Additional Expenses:

TOTAL AUGUST EXPENSES:

AUGUST NET PROFIT:
(Gross Sales Minus Expenses)

AUGUST MILEAGE:

SEPTEMBER 2020

LISTING GOALS	ACTUAL LISTINGS

SALES GOALS	ACTUAL SALES

NOTES:

September 2020

Sunday	Monday	Tuesday	Wednesday	Thursday	Friday	Saturday
30	31	1	2	3	4	5
6	7	8	9	10	11	12
13	14	15	16	17	18	19
20	21	22	23	24	25	26
27	28	29	30	1	2	3

_____

_____

_____

_____

SEPTEMBER BANK ACCOUNT LEDGER

CHECK #	DATE	TRANSACTION	DEBIT	CREDIT	BALANCE

SEPTEMBER BANK ACCOUNT LEDGER

CHECK #	DATE	TRANSACTION	DEBIT	CREDIT	BALANCE

SEPTEMBER MILEAGE

DATE	DESTINATION	TASK	MILES	TOTAL

SEPTEMBER MILEAGE

DATE	DESTINATION	TASK	MILES	TOTAL

SEPTEMBER COST OF GOODS (COGS)

DATE	LOCATION	CASH/CHECK/CARD	COST	TOTAL

SEPTEMBER COST OF GOODS (COGS)

DATE	LOCATION	CASH/CHECK/CARD	COST	TOTAL

SEPTEMBER INCOME REPORT
GROSS SALES

Amazon Sales:

Ebay Sales:

Etsy Sales:

Poshmark Sales:

Mercari Sales:

Facebook Sales:

Instagram Sales:

YouTube Sales:

Local Sales:

Other Sales:

TOTAL SEPTEMBER GROSS SALES:

SEPTEMBER INCOME REPORT - EXPENSES

Amazon Fees:
Ebay Fees:
Etsy Fees:
Poshmark Fees:
Mercari Fees:
PayPal Fees:
Additional Fees:

Cost of Goods:
Postage:
Advertising:
Office/Shipping Supplies:
Equipment:
Phone/Internet:

Sales Tax:
Business Insurance:
Health Insurance Premiums:
Prescription Drugs:
CoPays/Deductibles:

Travel:
Meals:
Additional Expenses:

TOTAL SEPTEMBER EXPENSES:

SEPTEMBER NET PROFIT:
(Gross Sales Minus Expenses)

SEPTEMBER MILEAGE:

OCTOBER 2020

LISTING GOALS

ACTUAL LISTINGS

SALES GOALS

ACTUAL SALES

NOTES:

October 2020

Sunday	Monday	Tuesday	Wednesday	Thursday	Friday	Saturday
27	28	29	30	1	2	3
4	5	6	7	8	9	10
11	12	13	14	15	16	17
18	19	20	21	22	23	24
25	26	27	28	29	30	31

OCTOBER BANK ACCOUNT LEDGER

CHECK #	DATE	TRANSACTION	DEBIT	CREDIT	BALANCE

OCTOBER BANK ACCOUNT LEDGER

CHECK #	DATE	TRANSACTION	DEBIT	CREDIT	BALANCE

OCTOBER MILEAGE

DATE	DESTINATION	TASK	MILES	TOTAL

OCTOBER MILEAGE

DATE	DESTINATION	TASK	MILES	TOTAL

OCTOBER COST OF GOODS (COGS)

DATE	LOCATION	CASH/CHECK/CARD	COST	TOTAL

OCTOBER COST OF GOODS (COGS)

DATE	LOCATION	CASH/CHECK/CARD	COST	TOTAL

OCTOBER INCOME REPORT
GROSS SALES

Amazon Sales:

Ebay Sales:

Etsy Sales:

Poshmark Sales:

Mercari Sales:

Facebook Sales:

Instagram Sales:

YouTube Sales:

Local Sales:

Other Sales:

TOTAL OCTOBER GROSS SALES:

OCTOBER INCOME REPORT - EXPENSES

Amazon Fees:
Ebay Fees:
Etsy Fees:
Poshmark Fees:
Mercari Fees:
PayPal Fees:
Additional Fees:

Cost of Goods:
Postage:
Advertising:
Office/Shipping Supplies:
Equipment:
Phone/Internet:

Sales Tax:
Business Insurance:
Health Insurance Premiums:
Prescription Drugs:
CoPays/Deductibles:

Travel:
Meals:
Additional Expenses:

TOTAL OCTOBER EXPENSES:

OCTOBER NET PROFIT:
(Gross Sales Minus Expenses)

OCTOBER MILEAGE:

NOVEMBER 2020

LISTING GOALS

ACTUAL LISTINGS

SALES GOALS

ACTUAL SALES

NOTES:

November 2020

Sunday	Monday	Tuesday	Wednesday	Thursday	Friday	Saturday
1	2	3	4	5	6	7
8	9	10	11	12	13	14
15	16	17	18	19	20	21
22	23	24	25	26	27	28
29	30	1	2	3	4	5

NOVEMBER BANK ACCOUNT LEDGER

CHECK #	DATE	TRANSACTION	DEBIT	CREDIT	BALANCE

NOVEMBER BANK ACCOUNT LEDGER

CHECK #	DATE	TRANSACTION	DEBIT	CREDIT	BALANCE

NOVEMBER MILEAGE

DATE	DESTINATION	TASK	MILES	TOTAL

NOVEMBER MILEAGE

DATE	DESTINATION	TASK	MILES	TOTAL

NOVEMBER COST OF GOODS (COGS)

DATE	LOCATION	CASH/CHECK/CARD	COST	TOTAL

NOVEMBER COST OF GOODS (COGS)

DATE	LOCATION	CASH/CHECK/CARD	COST	TOTAL

NOVEMBER INCOME REPORT
GROSS SALES

Amazon Sales:

Ebay Sales:

Etsy Sales:

Poshmark Sales:

Mercari Sales:

Facebook Sales:

Instagram Sales:

YouTube Sales:

Local Sales:

Other Sales:

TOTAL NOVEMBER GROSS SALES:

NOVEMBER INCOME REPORT - EXPENSES

Amazon Fees:
Ebay Fees:
Etsy Fees:
Poshmark Fees:
Mercari Fees:
PayPal Fees:
Additional Fees:

Cost of Goods:
Postage:
Advertising:
Office/Shipping Supplies:
Equipment:
Phone/Internet:

Sales Tax:
Business Insurance:
Health Insurance Premiums:
Prescription Drugs:
CoPays/Deductibles:

Travel:
Meals:
Additional Expenses:

TOTAL NOVEMBER EXPENSES:

NOVEMBER NET PROFIT:
(Gross Sales Minus Expenses)

NOVEMBER MILEAGE:

DECEMBER 2020

LISTING GOALS

ACTUAL LISTINGS

SALES GOALS

ACTUAL SALES

NOTES:

December 2020

Sunday	Monday	Tuesday	Wednesday	Thursday	Friday	Saturday
29	30	1	2	3	4	5
6	7	8	9	10	11	12
13	14	15	16	17	18	19
20	21	22	23	24	25	26
27	28	29	30	31	1	2

DECEMBER BANK ACCOUNT LEDGER

CHECK #	DATE	TRANSACTION	DEBIT	CREDIT	BALANCE

DECEMBER BANK ACCOUNT LEDGER

CHECK #	DATE	TRANSACTION	DEBIT	CREDIT	BALANCE

DECEMBER MILEAGE

DATE	DESTINATION	TASK	MILES	TOTAL

DECEMBER MILEAGE

DATE	DESTINATION	TASK	MILES	TOTAL

DECEMBER COST OF GOODS (COGS)

DATE	LOCATION	CASH/CHECK/CARD	COST	TOTAL

DECEMBER COST OF GOODS (COGS)

DATE	LOCATION	CASH/CHECK/CARD	COST	TOTAL

DECEMBER INCOME REPORT
GROSS SALES

Amazon Sales:

Ebay Sales:

Etsy Sales:

Poshmark Sales:

Mercari Sales:

Facebook Sales:

Instagram Sales:

YouTube Sales:

Local Sales:

Other Sales:

TOTAL DECEMBER GROSS SALES:

DECEMBER INCOME REPORT - EXPENSES

Amazon Fees:
Ebay Fees:
Etsy Fees:
Poshmark Fees:
Mercari Fees:
PayPal Fees:
Additional Fees:

Cost of Goods:
Postage:
Advertising:
Office/Shipping Supplies:
Equipment:
Phone/Internet:

Sales Tax:
Business Insurance:
Health Insurance Premiums:
Prescription Drugs:
CoPays/Deductibles:

Travel:
Meals:
Additional Expenses:

TOTAL DECEMBER EXPENSES:

DECEMBER NET PROFIT:
(Gross Sales Minus Expenses)

DECEMBER MILEAGE:

2020 INCOME REPORT
YEAR-END GROSS SALES

Amazon Sales:

Ebay Sales:

Etsy Sales:

Poshmark Sales:

Mercari Sales:

Facebook Sales:

Instagram Sales:

YouTube Sales:

Local Sales:

Other Sales:

TOTAL 2020 GROSS SALES:

2020 INCOME REPORT YEAR-END EXPENSES

Amazon Fees:
Ebay Fees:
Etsy Fees:
Poshmark Fees:
Mercari Fees:
PayPal Fees:
Additional Fees:

Cost of Goods:
Postage:
Advertising:
Office/Shipping Supplies:
Equipment:
Phone/Internet:

Sales Tax:
Business Insurance:
Health Insurance Premiums:
Prescription Drugs:
CoPays/Deductibles:

Travel:
Meals:
Additional Expenses:

TOTAL 2020 EXPENSES:

2020 NET PROFIT:
(Gross Sales Minus Expenses)

2020 MILEAGE:

Made in the USA
Columbia, SC
24 January 2021